CRIME AND SEX IN HANDWRITING

By the same author

Graphology

Patricia Marne

CRIME AND SEX
IN HANDWRITING

NEW CENTURY PUBLISHERS, INC.

Printing Code
11   12   13   14   15   16

ISBN 0-8329-0149-0

With acknowledgements to
ALEC HARRISON and ELEANOR EASOM

Contents

Contents

Contents 9

Contents

Introduction

Although the Ancient Chinese and Romans accepted that there was a relationship between handwriting and personality, it was not until comparatively recently that graphology could lay claim to being a science, following clearly defined rules, and producing findings accurate enough to be used in personnel work in the professions, and in commerce and industry, to assess character and suitability. Furthermore, serious practitioners have had to fight against popular misconceptions that associate graphology with fortune-telling and forecasting the future.

Until the late middle ages learning to write had been the prerogative of monks and the aristocracy and, though there was a steady evolution of basic principles, it was not until the practice of writing became part of everyday life that graphology started to come into its own.

Some two hundred years ago graphologists were of two schools: one intuitive, the other analytical. The first would assess handwriting from the general impression it gave (its 'form level'), while the second studied what they termed 'isolated signs' and individual idiosyncrasies of letter formation.

Gradually these two were integrated and in the nineteenth century psychologists such as Max Pulver and Carl Jung added a new dimension to graphology by seeing symbols in handwriting which could reveal the subconscious drives of the writer. Today, as a result of this and other researches, it is accepted that handwriting can get nearer the truth about an individual than shrewd, sympathetic questioning.

Because graphology reveals the submerged personality, the hidden weaknesses and strengths of the writer, it enables the graphologist to determine with authority the character of the writer, his disposition, educational development, emotional and mental faculties and the influences that may affect him from both emotional and environmental experiences. The graphologist is able to interpret quickly and objectively, often confirming the opinion of psychologists and criminologists.

Graphology at work

This book is concerned with two specialised areas: criminal tendencies and sexual inclinations as revealed in handwriting. These are shown by a wide variety of tell-tale signs, but no graphologist would describe a person 'dishonest' or 'lecherous' just on the strength of one or two of these give-away clues, any more than a physician would diagnose a particular illness without taking more than one symptom into account.

Even when the presence of a particular characteristic has been confirmed, the graphologist will balance it against other characteristics. A particular handwriting may show clear signs that two individuals are thieves. But further study will show that one is aggressive and the other is not. One, if caught will attack and seriously injure his detector; the other will concede 'It's a fair cop' and go quietly.

In the second field, there may be unmistakable signs that two men each have a strong sex drive. One may be a demanding but faithful husband; the other could be a rapist.

In each of these instances, a careful study of the handwriting of each of these four men will reveal the differences. It is unwise, therefore, to form a hasty assessment.

Before venturing into these two specialised fields it will be helpful first to define very briefly the basic technical know-how which graphologists apply when studying any script.

All handwriting analysis is based on three zones:

Upper
Middle   *graphology*
Lower

The upper zone shows the spiritual and intellectual state,

the middle zone the social and day-to-day attitude, and the lower zone the materialistic and subconscious instincts: emotional and sex drives. Ideally each zone should be the same size but this rarely happens. Where it does, the writing may seem dull and stereotyped.

If there is neglect of one zone or an exaggeration at the cost of others, this has a special significance and has to be taken into account.

Two factors which handwriting does not reveal with absolute certainty are age and gender. Before attempting an analysis, it is important to know these because some people at twenty are more mature than others at fifty. Everyone, too, has male and female characteristics in different proportions, both physically and psychologically.

Having noted the three zones, the graphologist then looks for further clues in:

The slant
Pressure and speed
Script size and formation
Base line (whether straight or wavering)
Form level, (whether high, medium, or low) – this is
    important for revealing intelligence
Margins
Spacing, between letters, words and lines
Capital letters
Small letters
The capital *I* and letter *t* bar crossing
Loops, or lack of them
Punctuation marks
Signature
Numerals

There are, of course numerous finer points but where relevant they are mentioned later in following chapters.

Part 1
Crime and handwriting

Graphology and the law

Just as fingerprints studied by an expert can reveal the identity of a suspect, handwriting, when analysed by an experienced graphologist, can provide unmistakable clues in detecting criminal tendencies. Handwriting and fingerprints are both unique to the owner, but it has taken the judiciary in Britain longer to accept the value of graphology as evidence than it has in Europe. Scotland Yard and the C.I.D. of many other police forces will consider any leads when painstakingly sifting clues in tracking down wrong-doers, but rarely do they acknowledge publicly that they employ graphologists, preferring to call them handwriting experts.

This use of graphology by criminologists is by no means new, and there are many instances over the years, as this book will show, where the study of handwriting has been used to reveal criminal or anti-social tendencies of men and women in notorious cases, the most recent being the analysis of the script of writers, usually anonymous, and sometimes hoaxers, in the 'Yorkshire Ripper' investigation.

Clues to criminal types

Open baseline to small a's and o's

A cardinal sign of deceit is the open baseline to the small *a*'s and *o*'s. This is not only a sign of dishonesty but of hypocrisy, and shows the writer is not to be trusted. In this illustration the left slant and the thick pasty writing also point to dishonesty. The short heavy *t* bar crossing indicates a bad temper and the arcade writing of the small *m*'s and *n*'s (see page 23) are an added sign of a person who is deceitful.

Wavering baseline

The wavering baseline with its ups and downs and words running into each other, shows an erratic and disorderly mind, with inner conflict, and an individual who is anything but calm and composed. The writer is disturbed emotionally and the downward slope towards the end of the lines shows depression and pessimism.

Variable slant

A varying slant means that the writer, although versatile, quickly loses interest and is erratic and mercurial. The *a*'s and *o*'s open at the top show that he is likely to be over-active, over-talkative and over-react in situations that call for self-control.

Inflated capitals

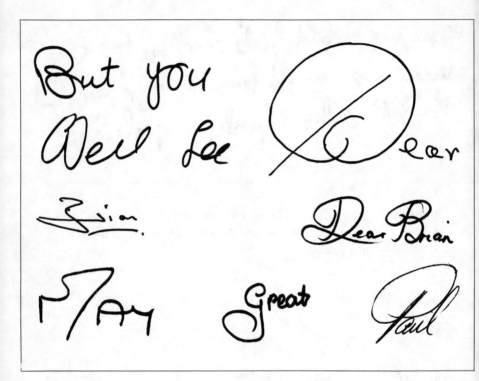

Inflated or exaggerated capitals are seen in the handwriting of people who love to be admired and who enjoy being the centre of attention. The egoist who seeks the limelight, the weak-willed and the inferiority complex are often hidden behind huge embellished capitals; they indicate the writer is far more interested in giving an impression, in showing off at all costs, even employing deceit at times, rather than in being himself. They also have neurotic tendencies, as these capitals frequently show a narcissistic desire for grandeur, a weakness many criminals have.

Left tending strokes to capitals

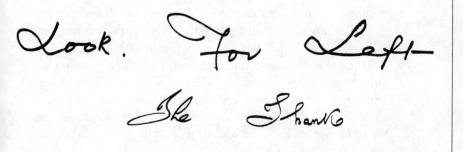

Left tending strokes to capitals again indicate deceitfulness. When seen frequently, with long loops and reaching far to the left, it is an unmistakable sign of dishonesty.

This deceit may not always be criminal deceit but emotional, and it indicates a fair amount of vanity on the part of the writer.

Enrolled capitals

These are a cardinal sign of deceit.

Signatures

If the signature is the same size as the rest of the script, this is usually a sign of reliability and honesty, and a desire to communicate clearly and distinctly. The writer does not put up any façade but is the same in private as in public.

When there is a discrepancy between signature and script and the signature is entirely different from the body of the writing, this can denote a dual nature and shows that the writer hides behind a mask and conceals his inner nature. See the signatures of Emil Savundra (p. 30) and Charles Manson (p. 62).

Thread script

This threadlike writing shows the opportunist, someone who knows how to manipulate and persuade, and also someone difficult, if not impossible, to pin down. Such writers are versatile, changeable, and possess considerable talent for getting on with people, and the ability to get their own way. They are quick thinking and able to make decisions.

They are all things to all people, and among these scripts we have the man who can adapt to any situation and turn it to advantage.

This script is found among shrewd opportunists who are also clever and creative. But it may also be that of the dishonest salesman, the con man, the quick-witted, get-rich-quick businessman who preys on the gullible.

Arcade writing

When letters are arched at the top in arcade fashion (note the small *m*'s and *n*'s) they reveal a personality who prefers to keep his thoughts to himself and is secretive, not necessarily to deceive, but through habit. The higher the arcade the more artistic the writer, the flatter the arcade the more of an intriguer. Arcade script which slants to the left reveals deceit, and this example also has a symbol of the pound sign, showing more than a passing interest in money.

Flat small m's

Small flat-topped *m*'s and *n*'s reveal the bluffer, the person who can usually talk or act his way out of difficult situations and who is lacking in normal moral standards.

This wide script shows extravagance and a lack of appreciation of the value of time or effort in everyday affairs. This and the light pressure shows the writer to be hyper-sensitive and critical of others.

Liar's t bar crossing

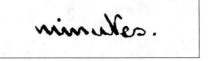

This *t* bar coming down the stem and going over to the right shows the writer who will not hesitate to lie or use deceit to extricate himself from awkward situations in which he is at fault. The habitual liar often repeats this *t* bar throughout his script. In graphology this is regarded as one of the most revealing signs.

Touching up strokes

Touching up and going over the strokes show a neurotic personality, full of uncertainty, lacking in decisiveness and unreliable. These are not necessarily criminal traits but the obsessive necessity to add, strengthen or make legible his writing is a sign of neurosis caused by inner conflicts and anxiety.

Letters omitted

Letters that are omitted in handwriting reveal a poor memory and sometimes nervousness or anxiety. They are also seen in handwriting of dishonest people, and these slips of the pen may stem from inner conflicts – usually of guilt, as the writers are constantly on the lookout for detection.

Pasty writing

Pasty writing shows sensuality and is found in the handwriting of those who allow their appetites to rule, to indulge in excessive eating, drinking and sex. It shows a preoccupation with the physical and reveals the force of energy the writer uses. When the writing is light and pasty the vitality is less than when it is heavy and muddy in appearance.

Uneven (periodic) pressure

Uneven or periodic pressure reveals irritability and a very uncertain temper under tension. The writer is easily excited and stimulated, and can be demanding in the sexual erotic area. Lack of emotional balance is also indicated, resulting sometimes in violent behaviour according to the heaviness of the pressure.

Split letters

dont ever seem to
get things done.

Letters that are split apart show dishonesty in money affairs. When accompanied by a left slant and arcade script, they are signs to be watched as the writer will also distort the truth. This sign shows weakness of will due to nervous anxiety and feelings of guilt.

Examples

The criminally dishonest

> way about the job, I cant see how I am
> going to make much of a success of it,

This writer's script shows four cardinal signs of dishonesty. Left slant, arcade *m*'s and *n*'s, an open base for the small *a*'s and *o*'s and enrolled capitals.

The large loop to the small *h* reveals a slightly muddle-headed personality, and the slow ponderous writing a lack of mental agility.

Emil Savundra (see p. 30 for illustration)

Savundra was a financier who spent several years in prison in connection with insurance frauds. An outstanding characteristic of his writing is the discrepancy between the signature and the text. The small writing shows mental agility, the exaggerated capital *I* his ego, and the large upward-rising underlined signature shows his self-love, ambition and desire for greatness, prestige and position.

in Parliament some weeks ago!

I may be released on parole at any time.
At the other extreme I might even have to fight
my way out of prison by the processes of "habeas corpus" etc.
around mid-June 1973.

In either case, may I contact you or
one of your colleagues when I am free again,
with a view to a possible meeting?

One thing alone is certain — Motor insurance
CAN be made profitable, IMMEDIATELY, and
right from the "OFF", on a massive
commercial scale — even on a European basis!

Yours Sincerely,

[signature]

The criminally insane

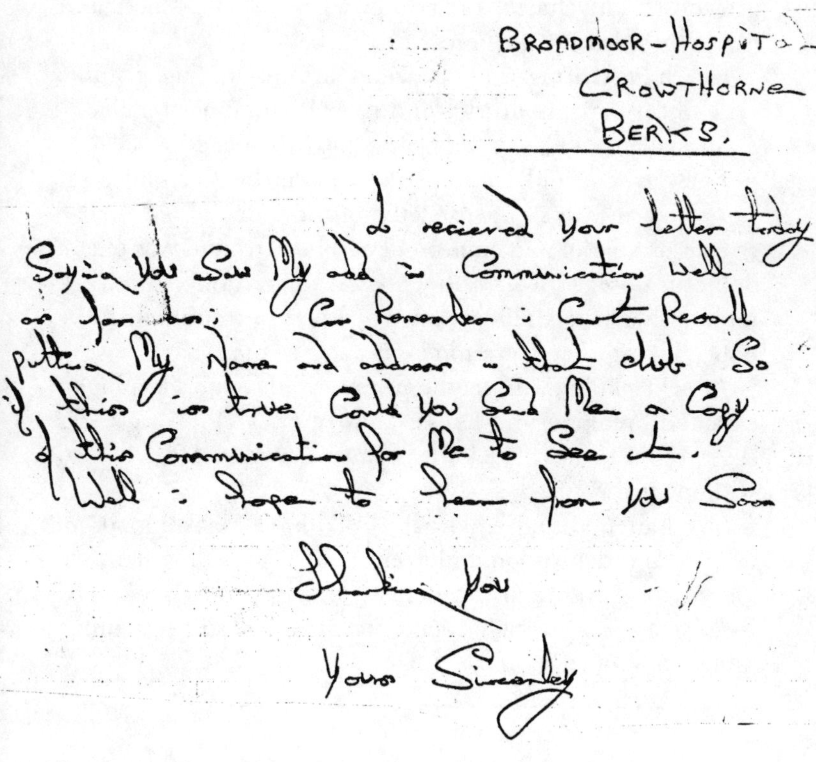
BROADMOOR-HOSPITAL
CROWTHORNE
BERKS.

I recieved your letter today
Saying You Saw My add in Communication well
as far as I Can Remember I Can't Recall
putting My Name and address in that club So
if this is true Could You Send Me a Copy
of this Communication for Me to See it.
Well I hope to hear from You Soon

Thanking You

Yours Sincerely

This writer was judged criminally insane. The curious unusual upper loops, nicked and slanting to the left show he is unrealistic and does not come down to earth.

Such a person lives in his own private world of fantasy, often in a state of exaltation for which there is lack of reason or logic. The large and frequent use of capitals is often seen in the handwriting of writers suffering from delusions of grandeur or megalomania. The writers lack all sense of proportion and rarely leave the institutions where they live out their fantasies.

The psychopathic criminal

This woman aged 23 has a history of violence, including grievous bodily harm, breaking and entering, assault and carrying a deadly weapon.

Her handwriting and drawings are fascinating graphic symbols of her immaturity and psychopathic personality.

She killed an eleven-year-old child when she herself was just eleven years old, stabbing the other girl with a knife, but ran away and was not suspected of the crime.

Her emotional and environmental background was one of domestic upsets, rows, arguments, a drunken father and weak mother, neglected children, two brothers in trouble with the police before they were nine, and aggression.

After the killing, she left home and lived rough, sleeping in cars and breaking into houses and factories . . . always – as she stressed – carrying a knife because she did not feel dressed without it.

She had nightmares about the killing, black moods of despair and depression and even thought of ending her own life. She was eventually apprehended, and sent to Borstal. At the age of 21 she was a hardened criminal and still very much hung up about the murder.

I'm sat on my bunk. Everything in my cell is very still. I like it in here. Without anyone ragging me, and prodding my mind. I just sit here in my fantasy **HIDE** looking at these bars keeping me in. I don't suppose if they weren't on I'd run. **IN MY SHELL** **I IMAGINE**

Some of her drawings illustrate her fears and terror depression and guilt, her persecution complex and her schizoid nature.

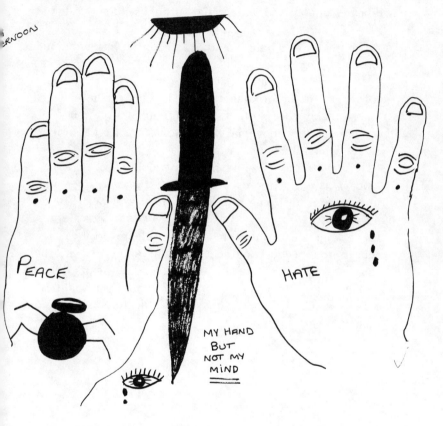

Her writing with its copybook form level and lack of originality shows immaturity and this is also revealed in the underlengths to her small *g* and *y* with their leftward swing. This shows her impressionability and lack of maturity.

The flat wide small *m*'s and *n*'s are a sign that she is not forthcoming and is able to bluff her way out of uncomfortable situations. The loops to the small *k* indicate rebelliousness. The fullness of a few upper loops shows that she is capable of emotion but the slanting to the left prevents her from expressing this easily.

There is a lack of consistency in the periodic pressure which indicates sudden and unexpected outbursts of temper due to frustration.

The fluctuating base line and slant reveal her emotional and mental instability.

However, the capital *I*, straight down and without any embellishment or ornamentation, shows that she can get down quickly to essentials and sum up a situation. The elongated dashes above the *i* stem show a quick and sensitive temper which flares up hastily.

Her preoccupation with knives is symbolic of her disturbed mind. This symbol is repeated over and over again, sometimes heavily dripping with blood, nearly always heavily filled in and with heavy pressure.

The anger, frustration and feelings of unworthiness are seen in the beetles, and despair and depression in the watching eyes which are an indication of suspicion. These frequently appear in the doodles of paranoid personalities.

This woman is pre-occupied with death, destruction, suicide, anger and hate.

A gallery of murderers

Because murder is the ultimate crime that one person can commit against another, it arouses deeper interest and curiosity – not always morbid – because people are intrigued about the personality of the killer. Although graphology can reveal the character and motivation of a killer, there is no such thing as 'a murderer's handwriting'.

Every person who kills for whatever purpose has an entirely different script – there are no two handwritings the same – but there are certain specific signs that point to possible future violence. For instance, ungovernable rage, hot temper and sadistic tendencies are all characteristics that can be seen in the script as warning signs.

The rape murderer will reveal strong sexual desires (see Cambridge rapist) which cannot be controlled, but each murderer is an individual whose handwriting must be examined to determine just what inner compulsion resulted in the taking of a life.

Most murders are domestic murders committed within the family in a moment of anger or passion, and by ordinary people. Until recently there were few murders in this country committed during robbery, but now this crime is on the increase, and a new ruthless kind of killer for gain is emerging. Whether murderers belong to the first category or the second does not mean that they have the same or similar handwriting.

The psychopath is perhaps the most cold-blooded of all murderers because he may have little motive for killing and will exhibit no sense of guilt.

His handwriting often shows extreme tension, anger and pent-up emotional rage that can smoulder quietly for years without erupting. His external attitude may be pleasant and normal on the surface, hiding his inner aggression so well that he is rarely suspected of being the anti-social person that he is. His handwriting will have positive traits as well as negative, and he is, of all criminals, the hardest to detect even from his handwriting.

He is mentally ill but not insane, and this definition is by itself confusing. His handwriting will reveal characteristics that taken together point to immaturity, emotional isolation and preoccupation with self, a low tolerance level, strong feelings of rejection, an abnormal interest in sex, and a lack of identity, all characteristic traits of the psychopathic killer.

Very often there are other clues in the form of strong emotional and environmental hang-ups from past experiences, usually of rejection by one or both parents in the formative years.

John George Haigh

Haigh was known as The Acid Bath Murderer because of his method of disposing of his victim's bodies in a bath of acid. He was hanged in Brixton Prison in 1946 and was believed to have killed at least five people for their money and property.

His handwriting at first sight is attractive, being well spaced, smooth and flowing, but closer examination gives a different picture. The thread formations show his talent for manipulating people for his own ends, and his capacity for being all things to all men.

He was not highly sexed, as demonstrated by the straight downstrokes of his *g*'s and *y*'s while the upright script indicates that his head ruled his heart and that he had plenty of self-control. The open small *a*'s and *o*'s are a sign of eloquence.

The fluctuating pressure nevertheless, shows instability and that the writer was living under considerable tension.

The 'garland' script (as the *m* in 'family') shows his almost

But there is no good
in my exposing that
thought as nobody
ever understands me.

You will doubtless have
told you that I have
arranged for patent
renewal fees and
all matters thereto to
be cared for for so
long as I am unable
to do so personally.

Also the Walpole
Investment Trust.

It is with joy that I
remember those
heavens that I have
known in the many
happy days that I
have spent with you:
the most wonderful

family that any man
could be privileged
to know.

My love to you all
John.

feminine personality and indicates that he could get along
well with elderly women.

His signature shows that he was subject to strong environmental and emotional influences from the past, and that he
was still affected by these links and ties. His enrolled small *s*'s
show shrewdness and a calculating mind.

Haigh was a clever and shrewd opportunist who was also a
strategist . . . in murder.

William Corder

Perpetrator of the infamous Red Barn murder; named thus
because the victim, Maria Martin, was found buried in the
barn in Polstead, Suffolk. Corder made a written confession
before he was hanged on 11th August 1828 in front of the gaol
at Bury St Edmunds, before a huge crowd.

The blotchy script shows sensuality and the varying
pressure indicates unpredictable moods. The long *t* bars that
cover the entire words, show a domineering and forceful
nature, and the angular formations of many small letters,
particularly the *n* and *m*, indicate aggression and energy. The
spacing is small and rushes towards the right margin,
indicating that he had an almost pathological need to be with

Colchester
George Inn
Wednesday
night 10 Oclock —

Dear Mother
I scarcely dare
presume to address you
having a full knowledge
of the shame disgrace
and I never truly owe
for ever to others upon
my family friends and late
formed connections; have
but few minute to write
and being unfortunately
labouring under this
serious charge. have to
solicit that you will
receive Mr. _____ on
friday morning with my
probable may for my injur'd
lawfull and I must do the
the justice to say with
affectionate wife

people. The high aggressive stroke to his capital *M* in Mother, confirms his aggressiveness.

William Gardiner

William Gardiner was a Suffolk carpenter, a rather pious Elder of the Methodist church, nicknamed Holy Willie, but gossip linked him with Rose Harsent, a 23-year-old maid in the household of a Baptist deacon. As a result he was summoned to appear before the church elders.

Rose was subsequently found dead, her throat cut and her body partly burned. A medicine bottle with traces of paraffin and bearing the names of two of Gardiner's children was found, and in Rose's bedroom an unsigned note of assignation. She was six months pregnant.

Gardiner was tried in Ipswich in 1902. His wife swore he was with her all through the night of the murder, save for half an hour, at about 11.30 p.m. She said she had given the medicine bottle containing camphorated oil to Rose, who had a cold. The Jury failed to agree and a new trial was ordered. Again the jury could not agree and Gardiner was released.

> I will try to see you tonight at 12 o'clock at your place if you put a light in your window at 10 o'clock for about 10 minutes then you can take it out again. don't have a light in your room at 12 as I will come round to the back

The most important aspects of Gardiner's handwriting are its neatness, the small script, the regular spacing, all of which are evidence of a conventional normal person. But the threadlike strokes which almost dissolve are a cardinal sign of the opportunist and the personality who knows how to manipulate and get his own way. He was able to use his considerable elusiveness to gain his own ends and wriggle out of responsibility.

Dr William Palmer

Dr Palmer was the notorious English poisoner of possibly fourteen people. His trial in 1856 made legal history because the inquest into the death of his last victim returned a verdict of wilful murder against him even before he was arrested.

This led to the Palmer Act making it possible for an accused person to be tried in London if he was unlikely to get a fair trial in his own county. Palmer was subsequently hanged.

it is now ½ p 10 I have just
came home from Hall to
write you for I do of... you
my dearest I should have
been very unhappy had I
not have done so.
My dearest Annie I
purpose all being well
being with you tomorrow
about three & depend
upon it nothing but
ill health will ever
keep me away from
you — forgive me my
duck for not sending
you the paper last
night I really could
not help it — I... do

explain fully tomorrow
my dear remember I say
something about need to
work — you will be amused
My sweetest & loveliest
Annie I never was more
pleased with you in my
life than I was on Friday
afternoon last — it was
a combination of things
God bless you I hope we
may live together & love
each other for 50 years
to come — Excuse more
for I must go — till tomorrow
Accept my everlasting love
& believe me
            Ever your most affect[ionate]
Sunday Evg ¼ to 10   Wm Palmer
                    3 tomorrow

Palmer's middle zone handwriting shows his intellectual capacity for assessing facts. The thread script also reveals his talent for manipulating them. The lack of clear spacing between words is a sign of gregariousness. Unlike many murderers, he preferred to have people around him and was not a loner, but the long *t* bar roofing his words now and then is an indication of his patronising attitude to others. His wide right margin reveals apprehension about the future.

Hawley Harvey Crippen

Crippen was an American, born in Michigan in 1852, who qualified as a doctor, and who came to England in 1900, but his qualifications did not allow him to practise.

He and his mistress Ethel le Neve, who was disguised as a boy, had fled the country after Crippen was suspected of murdering his wife. They were detained on board ship following radio messages from London, the first time radio had ever been used in crime detection. Crippen was subsequently convicted and hanged. Ethel le Neve was acquitted.

The threadlike strokes in Crippen's writing show his talent for using people to his own advantage, and the very small capitals reveal an inferiority complex. But the right slant shows him to be sociable and able to communicate and mix with people. The formation of his small *g*'s with their pointed downstrokes, indicate his lack of domestic harmony.

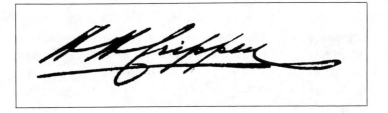

His signature with its right slant shows his passionate and ardent nature, and the heavier pressure used in this signature shows his desire for prestige and for people to think well of him.

Herbert Rowse Armstrong

Herbert Armstrong was a small town solicitor and retired British Army Major who was hanged in 1922 for the murder of his wife by poisoning.

His wife's death did not at first attract attention but later, when he attempted to poison a rival solicitor, his wife's body was exhumed and a post-mortem conducted by Bernard Spilsbury. The case aroused considerable public interest at the time.

His writing shows a very strong ego as evidenced in the larger than normal script signature, heavy underlining and

In replying to this letter, please write on the envelope:

Number   Name

Gloucester   Prison

30 May   1922

My dear Matthews.

My heart was too full today to say
all I wished. Thank you, my friend,
for all you have done for me. No one
could have done more. Please convey
also to all your staff my gratitude
for the unceasing work they put in.
No team could have worked more
loyally or with more devotion to duty

Ever your grateful friend

H Rouse Armstrong

with heavy pressure. This pressure shows his energy, while the thick *t* bar crossing indicates obstinacy and persistence which could find expression in an explosion of pent-up anger. He had a sadistic streak of refined brutality, as shown by the elongated *i* dots. The spacing shows the writer thinks first before acting and is capable of carefully and meticulously calculating his moves.

Ronald Bennell

Ronald Bennell, aged 18 years, was convicted in 1969 at Swanage, Dorset, for the rape and murder of 18-year-old Diana Stephanie Kemp.

This letter, written by Bennell, shows that he is semi-illiterate and extremely anxious. This is seen in the crossing out and over-stroking of letters. The varying slant and periodic pressure are indications of mental and emotional instability, and the large spacing between words shows that he is inclined to be a loner.

The writing also has a pastiness often seen in the script of the sexually excitable and sensual individual who has difficulty in keeping his instinctive urges under control.

William Herbert Wallace

Wallace was charged with the murder of his wife in 1930 in Liverpool. He was found guilty on circumstantial evidence, but on appeal he was cleared and left the court a free man. Wallace was 50, an insurance agent, quiet, inoffensive, intelligent and a member of the local chess club.

At first glance Wallace's handwriting is that of a well-balanced personality with mental alertness showing in the

I am completely satisfied that my call could not have been in better hands, and I know the amount of work put in by yourselves has been really great. What I do object to is that the damnable stupidity of the Lpool C.I.D. should have made it necessary. Still, I'm free again and that means everything.

I will get into touch with our Staff Federation and see what they have to say. You will I am sure realise that

I am anxious to have a settlement reached as early as possible and if there should be some slight delay I will do what I can to expedite matters.

With kindest regards.

Very sincerely yours

Wm. Wallace

small script and tidy spacing. But there are four other traits shown which are conflicting. He was timid and introverted, as shown in insignificant *I* revealing an inferiority complex. But he had a certain amount of concealed ego: the capital letters are inflated compared with the rest of the script, and the capital *M* with its downstroke turning right shows his vanity and that he would resent any interference in his affairs. The heavy *t* bar crossings going downwards are a sign of an aggressive, domineering and argumentative personality with an awkward temper under stress. The capital *B* is a significant sexual symbol in his writing, as it goes down into the lower zone. This, combined with the narrow downstrokes of his *g*'s and *y*'s, shows that he was sexually frustrated, and his emotional needs had been neglected. His handwriting provides some interesting sidelights into the personality of a complex character.

Charles Frederick Peace

Peace was one of the most notorious criminals and murderers of his age. He was born in 1832, was small, ugly but very agile and unusually strong. He became a master of disguise, and with theatrical flair he carried his housebreaking tools in a violin case. he shot a policeman and later the husband of a woman who had responded to his advances. He confessed to his crimes while awaiting execution, and was hanged in Leeds Prison in 1879. Many street ballads were written about him.

His script shows him to be almost illiterate, but the speed indicates a quick mind and ready wit. The high strokes to his small *p*'s show an enterprising nature and the long *t* bars, obstinacy and conceit. Some of the *t* bars have a symbolic shaped knife which reveal an unpredictable and unpleasant temper.

The uneven pressure is a sign of mood variation and instability. The *i* dot in the 'sir', in the form of a small arc, demonstrates his quick and acute perception.

The left swing of his small *g*'s and *y*'s reveal that in his early life there was a strong, maybe dominant, mother influence.

Lord Lucan

Lord Lucan is the peer the police want to interview following the murder of the nanny to his children in 1974.

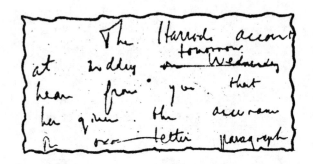

His small script reveals intelligence, and that he was under pressure at the time of writing. The overstrokes on some of his letters indicate neurotic tendencies, although the letters and their formations show self-control which may become weaker as feelings of persecution are magnified; this is seen in the widening left margin.

The threadlike script indicates his persuasive tongue and the knowledge of how to use it. The wavering pressure and ticklike stroke at the end of his downstrokes, show aggression and variation of his mood.

Dr Buck Ruxton

Dr Ruxton was a 37-year-old Parsee doctor who in 1928 set up house in Lancaster with Isabella van Ess, who called herself Mrs Buxton.

In 1935 Mrs Buxton and her maid disappeared. Ruxton reported that she had left him for another man. After the recovery of parts of their bodies, Ruxton was charged with their murder, found guilty and hanged at Strangeways Prison in 1936.

Ruxton's writing, with its heavy pressure and pasty script, reveals strong physical appetite. The thick *t* bars show brutal temper under tension and the formation of his capital *R*'s with their strokes going far down into the lower zone area indicates

his unwillingness to compromise and an adamant attitude.
The long stroke beginning the word 'Mary' shows inflated
egoism and conceit.

Donald Neilson (The Black Panther)

Donald Neilson, aged 38, was convicted of the murder of
Leslie Whittle in 1975. Neilson known as the Black Panther
after shooting a security guard, left behind in an abandoned
car several envelopes bearing his handwriting.

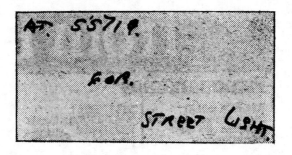

His writing is thick, with heavy pressure which shows
aggression and brutality, and he has an eccentric habit of
putting full stops between the letters when they are un-
necessary. His writing – in capitals – reveals fluctuating
pressure, which is a sign of emotional instability and often
anger. The overstroking of letters is a neurotic sign, which
with a wavering baseline shows a personality lacking in
balance to such an extent that the writer is dangerously anti-
social.

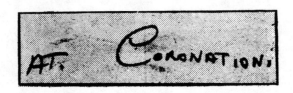

The large *C* shows that he has an exaggerated ego, while the pasty script reveals an earthy, materialistic nature. The

WALSAC

sharpness of the capital *L* at the end of Walsall is a sign of aggression as are the hooks on his capital *W*.

Jack the Ripper

This pasty, rather 'smudgy' or 'dirty' writing is from a letter believed to have been written by the original Whitechapel murderer known as 'Jack the Ripper'.

It is completely chaotic in form and erratic in rhythm. The long downstrokes to his small *g* and *y* are a sign of aggression, the periodic pressure reveals anger with emotional instability, leading to violent mood variation.

Old boss you was rite it was
the left kidny i was goin to
hoperate agin clos to your
ospitle just as i was goin
to drop mi nife along of
er bloomin throte them
cusses of coppers spoilt
the game but i guess i wil
be on the job soon and will
send you another bit of
innerds   jack the ripper

O have you seen the devle
with his mikerscope and scalpul
a lookin at a kidney
with a slide cocked up

The pointed *t* bars with their symbols of knives or daggers in the cross bar and their sharpening points indicate, and are symbolic of, the murder weapons used to mutilate victims. The 'blobbing' of the ink is a sign of sensuality. The muddled and jumbled lines with the letters running into each other demonstrate inability to control intense emotion.

Peter William Sutcliffe

Peter William Sutcliffe the 34-year-old Bradford lorry driver known as the 'Yorkshire Ripper' was jailed for life in May 1981 after being found guilty of murdering 13 women and attempting to murder 7 more.

Sutcliffe was sentenced to serve at least 30 years and to be released only on licence. Most of the women he killed were prostitutes, Sutcliffe claiming that he had a 'Divine mission' to slaughter them after hearing voices in a Bingley cemetery while working as a grave-digger.

His pleas of not guilty through diminished responsibility were rejected by a jury vote of 10 to 2.

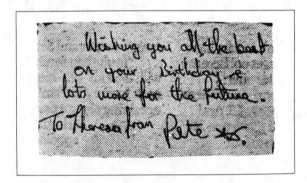

The left slant to Sutcliffe's handwriting reveals his introverted nature and shows that he leads an active inner life, is introspective, and from the pressure also suffers from depres-

ᴀRK TRANSPORT

EVERANCE IRONWORKS

'LEY

ıone 54031 day

598427 night

№ 06660

Date ~~COLLECT~~ / DELIVER

(delete when not applicable)

TINATION	DESCRIPTION
WᴬᴿD BLENKINSOP LTD HALEBANK FACTORY LOWER RD WIDNESS CHESHIRE	140 DRUMS CHEMICALS 77,42 KGS.

No. FᴿᴼM 2 KGS		Tons	Cwts	Qtrs	lbs
'ER'S NAME					
⁻ARRIVAL 8-10 Aᴹ					
DEP. 10-45.Aᴹ					
⁻TIMES 12·30-10 Pᴹ					

sion. The rising lines of the writing signify undue optimism at times.

The left slant also shows that he has strong emotional and environmental ties from his formative years which influence him and which he finds difficulty in breaking. He also has a strong attachment to his mother who had a lot of influence on him, leading to a curious love/hate relationship.

The lines going through his signature in a backward formation are highly significant as they reveal hostility to self – a cancelling out of the ego – and a suicide sign in graphology. Self-destructive urges are frequently found in handwriting either as a cry for help by the writer or as a genuine bid for death.

Paul John Knowles

Knowles was an American escaped convict, who killed at least fifteen people in a four-month period in 1975. All the victims were seemingly selected at random and most were killed brutally. After his arrest and whilst being transferred from one gaol to another, he managed to free one hand from his handcuffs and went for the driver's gun. Knowles was shot dead by one of the escorting police officers.

His writing shows a pronounced right slant showing his lack of emotional control and the strong leftward swing of his small g's indicate a mother complex leading to suppressed homosexual tendencies.

The writing is pasty which is a sign of sensuality and strong physical urges, and the whiplike strokes going up and over to the left on the ending of many words is a sign of self-blame and guilt . . . they also are symbolic of his liking for ropes to tie up his victims.

For Paul John Knowles' letter, see opposite.

Charles Manson

Charles Manson was the leader of the so-called 'Family' whose brutal killings in California in August 1969 were followed by a sensational trial, in which Manson and three girl followers were tried for seven murders. All four were found guilty and sentenced to death, which meant life imprisonment.

NATIONAL CREDIT CARD APPLICATION

UNION

Union Oil Company of California   Please print

For Credit Department use
PS
Cards 1 2 3 ___ Code T P
Approved by

Name (full first name, second initial, last name): *Charles M Manson* ✓   Age: 35   No. of dependents: 16   Wife's first name: none

Street address: 441 N. Bouchet   How long at address: 10 Mos   Own ☐ Buying ☐ Rent ☒

City, state and zip code: Los Angeles, Calif.   Social Security no.: 560-84-8462

Previous address (street, city, state): Spahn's Movie Ranch Chatsworth, Calif.   How long at address: 1 Years

Employer's name (if self employed, name of business): Evangalist   Type of business: Religious   Length of employment: 20 years

Business address (street, city, state):   Position: Monthly salary: 100-199 ☐ 400-499 ☐ 500-699 ☐ 700 & over ☒

Previous employer (if above employment is less than 2 years):   Position: Length of employment:

Wife's employer: Position: Monthly salary: Length of employment:

Credit is established with (include name of oil company credit cards and account number):

Name/address: George Spahn, Chatsworth   [ ] 30 Day [ ] Budget   Bank used: Republic National

Name/address: A Joint Venture 13150 Chandler Van Nuys, Calif.   [ ] 30 Day [ ] Budget   Branch: No Hollywood

Name/address: [ ] 30 Day [ ] Budget   Account no.:   ☒ Checking ☐ Savings

Number of cards desired: 2   Mail statements to: ☒ Residence ☐ Business   Applicant agrees to terms and conditions of use printed on credit card

Date: / /   Residence phone no.: 680-9600   Signature: *Charles M Manson*

PLEASE ALLOW APPROXIMATELY 4 WEEKS FOR CREDIT INVESTIGATION AND ISSUANCE

The pronounced left slant to Manson's writing reveals his basically introverted nature which is a barrier between himself and the real world.

The low *t* bars indicate a depressive personality and the discrepancy between his script and signature indicates his dual nature with an urge to be regarded as someone important. The small insignificant writing and the larger erratic and unstable signature without any rhythm to it show his personal imbalance. The angular strokes to his signature and narrow strokes are a sign of aggression and latent resentment.

Mark Chapman

Mark Chapman killed Beatle John Lennon in New York on 1st December 1980. Chapman, 25 years old and a security guard, was a Beatle fan and believed that *he* was Lennon and that the real Beatle was an impostor so shot him at point-blank range.

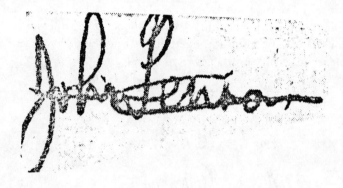

Chapman's 'Lennon' signature, with the lines scored through it, is a classic sign in graphology of the would-be-suicide. Hostility to self is shown by this cancelling out of the ego, and this type of graphic symbol is often seen in the handwriting of disturbed individuals. When the line is weak and does not go all the way through the signature, it can be a cry for help; when the signature is circled all the way round, it indicates strong suicidal and/or homicidal tendencies.

The inhibited letters and heavy pressure indicate his tension and highly emotional state at the time of writing.

William Heirens

Heirens, an American, brought up to believe that sexual relations were unclean, found sexual gratification in burglary and murder. By the age of thirteen he had committed eleven burglaries and set fire to six houses. As a student he regularly robbed apartments and later, in 1948, he killed two women and a six-year-old girl.

He confessed to reaching sexual climax during murder plus housebreaking. He was judged insane and sentenced to three consecutive life-terms, never to be released.

For heavens
sake catch me
Before I kill more
I cannot control myself

His childlike script, with downward slope and poorly formed letters, show emotional stress, nervousness and maladjustment.

Lee Harvey Oswald

Lee Harvey Oswald is thought to have been the killer of President Kennedy at Dallas in November 1963.

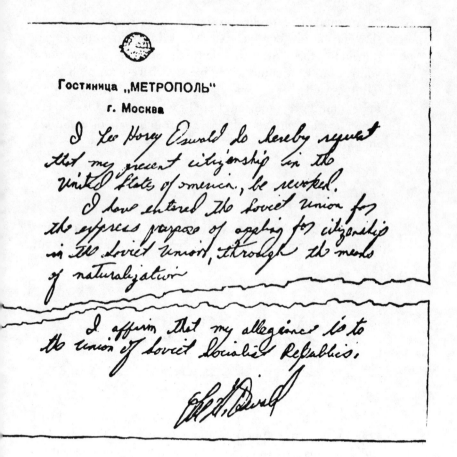

The pressure in Oswald's script varies, indicating emotional instability and inconsistency. The many different formations of his *t* bar crossings show indecisiveness and changing moods varying from undue optimism to depression and confusion.

The leftward swing of his small *g* and *y* and their underlengths indicate strong mother influence in his early years.

His small *d* is enrolled, a sign of his introspective nature, showing he is completely wrapped up in himself. His unusually forward right slant shows lack of emotional control, and the almost illegible signature with high upper loops, reveals his egoism and need to show off, seeking to appear far more important than he is. The name Oswald gets larger at the end and this is a cardinal sign of emotional immaturity.

Thomas Cochran

Thomas Cochran was convicted in the 1950s of murdering a young woman in South Florida, after posing as a movie scout.

He too has the pasty, sensual writing so often associated with abnormal sexual appetites and self-interest. The left slant indicates his introverted nature and the blobs reveal his sensuality.

H. Judd Grey

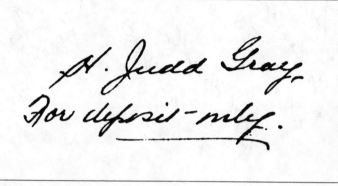

H. Judd Grey killed the husband of his lover in the 1950's,
and here again the muddy script reveals strong sexuality and
an exceedingly weak will. His forward right script indicates
an impulsiveness that led to the murder.

Constance Kent

Constance Kent, at 21 years old, confessed to killing her half-
brother five years earlier. She was suspected of murdering the
four-year-old at the time and was arrested, but later released
on her father's bond of £200. She entered a convent in France
and after two and a half years moved to a convent in
Brighton. Her religious beliefs led her to confess. She was sent
for trial at Salisbury Assizes in 1865, pleaded guilty and was
sentenced to death without a witness being called. The
sentence was commuted to life imprisonment and she was
released in 1885.

Even allowing for the flourishes to her script which were
popular and very much in evidence in handwriting in the last
century, this writing shows a healthy ego and a very strong
suppressed sexuality. The wide margin on the right is a sign of

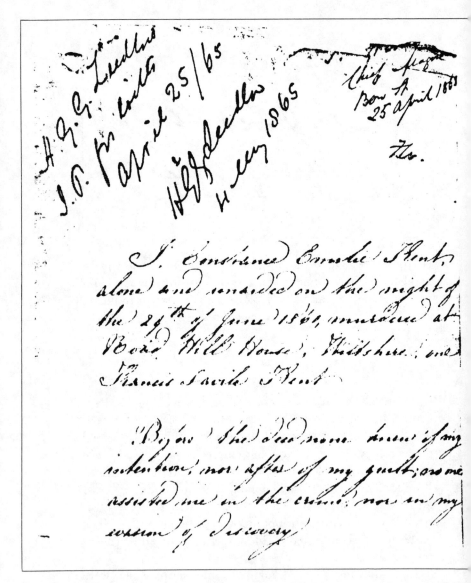

her fear about the past and indicates her desire to keep the world at bay as much as possible.

Excellent organising ability is shown in her spacing and the huge inflated capital reveals vanity and arrogance.

Myra Hindley

Hindley was imprisoned for life in May 1966 with her lover
Ian Brady, for the murder of Leslie Ann Downey aged ten,
and Edward Evans aged seventeen. She was convicted as an
accomplice to the murder of John Kilbride as well. The case
was known as 'The Moors Murders'.

Myra Hindley has an almost childlike script which is
legible and carefully formed. But the small size of her writing
and the capital *I* made in a single stroke down shows
intelligence and a quick grasp of essentials. She is able to
assess situations at a glance.

The left slant of her writing shows her to be basically

introverted yet the narrow spaces between her words demonstrate her need to be with people; this need is almost pathological.

The dots over the small *i* when elongated reveal touchiness and hyper-sensitivity under criticism. The light pressure of the writing is a sign of sensitivity. The middle zone letters because they are neglected, compared with the loops and underlengths, show that home and family feelings seem to be negative. The open underlengths to her small *g*'s and *y*'s indicate an extremely receptive and responsive personality in the erotic/sexual sphere, but one who is gullible and emotionally ambivalent. When the loop of the *g* and *y* are not crossed but open to the left, this is a sign of immaturity. The thick *t* bar crossing is an indication of obstinacy under tension. She is imaginative, responds to new ideas and projects, is capable of organised study or research and possesses persistence for sustained effort.

The rhythm of the writing looks reasonably stable until we look at the 'wavy' or slightly 'bent' formation of her upper loops. Even her small *h*'s and capital *I*s have this particular trait. This noticeable stroke is found in the handwriting of individuals suffering from mental disturbances or conflict due to anxiety. To the trained eye of the graphologist it indicates weakness of will and an easily led personality. A person who will take the easy way out of situations, who leads an active inner life hiding behind a camouflage like a chameleon, and adapts herself to every individual she contacts.

The fact that she does not join her letters in a normal manner, shows a desire to be different, to keep apart and conceal what she does not wish the world to see. The closed small *a*'s and *o*'s confirm her secretiveness.

Amelia Dyer

Amelia Dyer, in 1896, was responsible for the deaths by drowning of a number of young children near Reading. The thickness of her strokes reveals a brutal disposition, as does the pasty or muddy appearance of her letters in which the endings are abruptly cut off. Her motive was gain.

The hangman: Albert Pierrepoint

Albert Pierrepoint, the hangman, inherited his job from his father Henry and his uncle Tom and carried out the last ritual of his trade in 1956 when he retired for reasons that are still secret. A few years later the death penalty for murder in this country was abolished, and on the 23rd August 1964 the last two executions were carried out simultaneously in Liverpool and Manchester.

Pierrepoint was responsible for despatching many murderers to their death, among the most notorious Hanratty the A4 murderer, Christie the necrophiliac killer, Heath the sadist, Haigh the acid bath murderer, and Edith Thompson who was hanged with her lover Frederick Bywaters for the murder of her husband in 1923. The last woman to be hanged in Britain was Ruth Ellis in July 1955 for the shooting of her ex-lover.

Pierrepoint was also responsible for hanging many of the war criminals at Nuremburg.

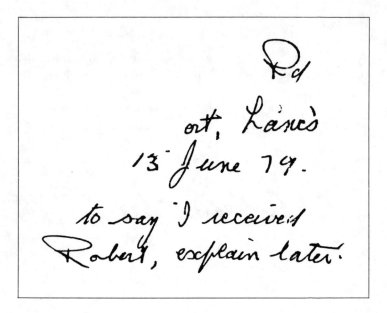

In the handwriting of this ex-public executioner the symbols of his trade can be seen in the noose formation in his upper loops on the letters *R* and *P*. He also forms his *t* bar crossing in a way that resembles a gallows.

The right slant of his script indicates that he is a socially minded man, with great self-reliance, he can be outward going and friendly but offset with a tinge of reserve, as he is, in fact, a very private person. He also shows in the large loop at the left of his capital *A* that he is a man proud of his family and his and their achievements.

Hoax letters

These hoax letters sent during the search for the so-called 'Yorkshire Ripper', indicate that the writer was a man of considerable energy and anger. This is seen in the heavy pressure, forward slant, and lack of control in the wavering baseline.

(reproduced smaller than actual size)

The straightforward *I* shows that his intelligence is above average, and he gets down to essentials quickly. The form level shows him to be a manual worker perhaps, or an artisan with a knowledge of the skill of writing.

(reproduced smaller than actual size)

The pointed downstrokes to his letters are a sign of aggression, and the varying slant indicates instability in the emotional area.

Political and war criminals

Benito Mussolini

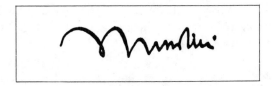

The left slant shows his introverted tendencies and that he was suppressed emotionally, while the pointed sharpness of his letters indicate his aggression and lack of tolerance. The repressed style of his script shows obsessional behaviour patterns, and those arcade formations indicate concealment and caution. He is not going to let anything stop him from achieving his aims. They also demonstrate suspicion and that he is under enormous pressure.

Adolf Hitler

The sample of Hitler's signature in 1933, just before he became Reich-Chancellor, has a tendency to fall downwards towards the end, indicating that he suffered from considerable depression, and was not a particularly optimistic personality.

Both this and his later signature, have a right slant with varying pressure and sharp knife-like crossings that also descend, emphasising his manic depressive state.

His signatures are made up of angles, always a sign of rigid and compulsive thinking, without care for the opinion or the views of other people.

There are signs of sudden and eruptive emotional outbursts in his writing, and in the second signature one can observe symbols of the SS, the emblem of Hitler's notorious bodyguard.

Heinrich Himmler

Even allowing for the fact that German writing is, and was even more so in the Thirties, much more angular and rigid than English script, Himmler has narrow and controlled angularity that shouts of aggression and a complete lack of warmth or emotion. The razor-like strokes breathe of intolerance and a calculated coldness with sadistic tendencies and an ability to carry orders out without qualm. This is a typical example of the schizoid personality.

Rudolf Hess

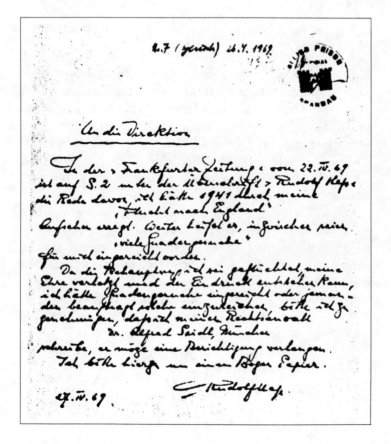

Compared with Himmler's signature, Hess has a far more rounded writing, a right slant, and better release of tension in the broader formations of his letters. he also reveals some altruism in the closeness of his words indicating his ability to work with others, and that he has a need to communicate.

There are no signs in his signature of the inbuilt sadism or aggression evident in Himmler's signature, and from his writing Hess shows a healthy respect for duty and conventionality.

Rapists

Crime statistics show that during the last ten years the number of cases of rape has shot up alarmingly, as has murder after rape. The handwriting of men who have committed this particular crime, not surprisingly, shows a strong sex drive which is revealed in the form of the small *g*'s and *y*'s (see Part Two: Sex and Handwriting) but it is difficult to generalise. There are countless men with a strong sex drive, but they have self-control and are not obsessed.

When these strong instinctive urges are seen in the handwriting of young people, their physical energy can be channelled into sport, games or other physical activities, and turned to good advantage. When this energy is repressed, it can erupt and lead to attacks on women.

When there is heavy pressure and pasty writing, it indicates someone more concerned with the purely sensual and physical, than light pressure.

Very often the rapist has strong latent homosexual tendencies – due to a mother fixation.

Peter Samuel Cook (The Cambridge Rapist)

Peter Samuel Cook, aged 47, was sent to prison in October 1975 after committing rape, and was found guilty on six charges of rape at Cambridge.

Cook had a history of crime since the age of ten, and had many convictions for burglary. He was sent to Broadmoor in 1966, was released two years later and went to live in Cambridge. He got married but his wife knew nothing of his sexual urges.

In 1980 Cook tried to smuggle letters out of Parkhurst

H. M. PRISON,
St. LOYES,
BEDFORD.

3rd, November 1965

Dear Sir,

Sorry to have to write you a letter from a prison, but I am up to my neck in trouble.

I'm asking you a favour on behalf of my Solicitors, that would you give me a working report a reference if you like.

Either I am a bad bricklayer or a good one. I know I had my ups and downs with the firm. But I was not sacked, I left and went on for Monks, Hills Road Bridge I think you will remember.

It would be greatly appreciated if you would do that for me. I always tried to do my best for the firm.

No. 244   (3301—3-10-62)

Prison on the Isle of Wight, to a national newspaper, in which he pleaded for assistance to obtain a sex-change operation. He also sent photographs of himself in female clothing. These pictures had been taken with a camera which had been smuggled into the prison.

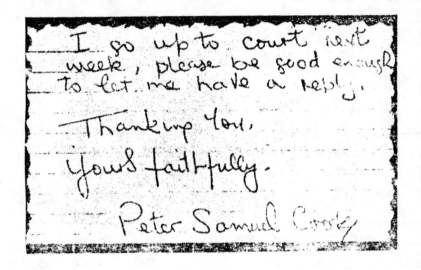

When we look at his handwriting, it is interesting to observe the traits that not only reveal his strong sexual urges but also female tendencies, and that he was from his youth under a strong female influence. These traits are often found in the handwriting of men with deep-rooted homosexual tendencies. They try to deny them and this leads in fact to them committing rape and assaults on women. This is often associated with a dominant mother influence. In fact Cook was very fond of his mother. The letter shown in the samples was written twelve years before he was committed for trial on charges of rape. The single signature was written at the time of the charges.

Anonymous letter writers

A skilful and fluent writer can quite easily assume a copybook hand and get away with it, but a slow and semi-literate writer can never disguise his lack of education by writing a quick and cultivated hand.

When an outbreak of anonymous letters occurs, one looks for motive words – that is names or words that have been written a little heavier than the rest of the script, and which obviously have a significant meaning to the writer. They can mean anger, hate, emotion or malice, but they do give away the writer's thoughts and indicate sometimes where the writer may be found, and why he or she has a grudge against someone and has to libel them.

The anonymous letter writer forgets that speed, pressure, spacing between words, letters, lines and margins, all reveal to the graphologist, with amazing accuracy, a lot about the writer's personality. When there are letters with which to compare the anonymous letters, then the culprit is quite easily spotted.

All the occupants of houses in an entire road of a London suburb received anonymous letters over a period of twenty years, causing considerable distress and misery to the recipients, many of whom were elderly or ill.

The letters were not obscene, or threatening, but lying, stupid and hurtful. Their malicious contents indicated the vicious nature of the mean and spiteful person who was penning them. An elderly woman was suspected by neighbours and the police were alerted, but they could do nothing as no one was seen actually to deliver the letters, as they were always posted from a nearby town.

The writing was compared with the script of the suspect and it was confirmed that she was indeed the anonymous letter writer. However, since she was old and ill she was not prosecuted.

The letters are reproduced here. They reveal the writer to be suffering from resentment, anger, frustration and jealousy and to be of slow and limited intelligence. The basic character structure of the writer is clear – the writing shows signs of senile decay, a narrow-minded hypersensitive personality with a highly developed critical sense.

The badly formed letters are a sign of a poorly educated writer with limited intelligence.

The pressure (in the animal welfare letter in particular) shows that it was written in extreme anger and under tension.

Please
see that your lovely cat is taken
in at night Im not saying the letter name
it wont cause any unpleasness I ask the
young lady near you because I thought
it was her cat she said no she has no pets
because of her mother.
I heard it wont stay in its not true its
has slept here with me for two days Im
moving and I wouldnt like to know its
neglected
                sorry its so lovely

WE THOUGHT YOU SHOULD NO THAT YOUR NEXT DOOR
NEIGHBOURS THERE NOT HUSBAND OR WIFE HE HAD A NICE
WIFE AND TWO CHILDREN HE LEFT HIS WIFE TO
LIVE WITH HER A AND SHE MADE HIM PUT
THEM IN DOCTOR BARNODOES HOME AND THEY
ARE TWO NICE CHILDREN SHE IS A BAD LOT SHE
IS A BOASTER TWISTER AND A FILTHY LIAR ALL
THAT HOME WHAT SHE AS GOT IS NOT PAID FOR
WE ALL NO WHAT SHE IS SHE HAD A GOOD
HUSBAND BUT HE WAS NOT ENOUGH FOR HER
SHE IS A EVIL WICKED JEALLOUS WOMAN SHE
CAN DRINK A BOTTLE OF JIN WHILE YOUR A
DRINKING A GLASS OF WATER WE ALL KNOW
HER OF OLD THEY ALL NO HER UP THE PRINCESS
BOUL IN FACT SHE IS WELL NOUN OVER GALE ST
AND HE IS NOT MUCH BETTER FOR HE AS A NASTY
NAME IN A WORKING MANS CLUB AT MILL RD
AVELEY AND A LOT OF CLUBS NO WHAT THEY
ARE ESPECIALY HER .

      SO SHE IS NOT A NEIGHBOUR FOR YOU.
FOR YOUR NICE PEOPLE, SWE ALL NO HER(

The script of the letter written in capitals demonstrates the immature nature of the writer; the letters increase in size at the end of words – a sign of immaturity – and under close scrutiny the letter formations show the same physically disintegrating strokes to be seen in the RSPCA letter.

The writer is living in a world of inner conflicts and partly because of her lack of physical energy and vitality she feels inadequate. Curiously, the rising lines show optimism and that the writer has an exaggerated ego that must be kept immaculate.

Your peter because you were 1st 8 76
an amateur prize fighter. buying a
few wines' beard you clouted an officer
of the law. you adopted a welsh name
I gather peter you could be a mixed breed
as in wales and england for generations
the suposed english and welsh scum
like your self are polish decent and
slave's Belguims and Balkan states the
man you assulted could be of the same
breed as you and a million welsh men
and if million in the english countries and
cities here in london they are all foriginers
say 8 cmillion you wereednunk when
you struck that policeman what were
you doing there any way you Bastard
you would not get away with it over
there in england you dirty low Bred
scum the foles in your church make
you are A ero Do me a favour peter
place you head in a gas oven or jump
under a Heavy Vehicle you and your
half Bred chinese jezzbe girl friend
I pray for your death you Bastard
you will not go there in a Hurry
again they should have escecuted
Both of you scum. I am writing the
government of that country when you
read this note you ll laugh peter alias Dewig
you one on the spot youldie soon
from I stefan you are not a penny Stint

This writer is extremely unbalanced as shown in the fluctuating slant and baseline. There are signs of a guilt complex, of aggression and hostility towards himself as seen in numerous swings to the left in the loops of the letters. The word 'executed' is, a little larger than the rest of his script, and is what is known as the motive word, emphasising his obsession with it.

He has found a way of expressing his resentment against everything and everybody in a negative way by putting pen to paper and writing abuse.

There are indications that the writer is a latent homosexual though it is possible that it was written by a masculine woman. The underlengths to the small *g* and *y* are swinging to the left – the mother fixation sign in graphology, and the open '*a*' and '*o*' indicate that he is talkative, needs to be with people, lacks discretion, and is obstinate to the point of stupidity.

The wavering base line shows his inconsistent personality and moodiness, being up one day and down the next, and also his nervous energy which finds expression in sudden bursts of irritability under tension.

Part 2
Sex and handwriting

Introduction

Graphology explodes as a myth the so-called 'sex symbols' because a study of their handwriting shows that very often they have a very low sex drive, and the image they present to the public is a carefully developed façade, fostered by shrewd and calculated publicity.

On the other hand, the writing of people who do not appear to be interested in sex often shows a strong sex drive and particular preferences in fulfilling these strong instinctive desires.

Nowhere is graphology more reliable than in giving a guide to the emotional and sexual compatibility of a couple in a relationship.

Revealing loops

Sexual drive, whether normal, subnormal or abnormal, is shown in handwriting by the formation of the small letters *g* and *y*. The small *f* and *j* are also pointers. The lower loops of these letters reveal the subconscious instincts, sexual preferences, drives and inclinations, and, if there are any, abnormalities.

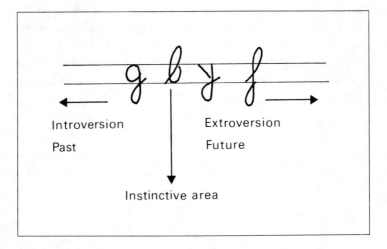

The way the *g* and *y* slant in the lower loops – left, right, or straight down – is significant. If the loop slants to the left, this is an indication of past emotional experiences (often of a mother complex) and the instincts are introverted and withdrawn. If the slant is to the right, this is an indication of a father influence. Lower loops that go straight down, loop and cross over, are called 'normal' in handwriting analysis.

The *g* and *y* should be studied, when possible, within words rather than when they fall at the end.

The small letter *f* which goes into the lower zone area also reveals sexual traits, particularly when formed with a triangular loop.

Another letter of the alphabet which reveals any sexual deviation is the capital *J*. In both male and female handwriting this can reveal homosexuality and is discussed more fully in a later chapter.

Why the letters *g* and *y* should show sexual traits in handwriting is not known. It is known, however, after years of research by well known graphologists and psychologists of repute, that they reveal with a remarkable degree of accuracy many sexual and emotional proclivities and inhibitions.

When a loop to the *g* or *y* is being formed, the impulse is to let the pen go downwards to form the stem and then finish the letter by bringing the pen smoothly upwards and over to form a loop.

The pen does not normally travel downwards unless there is a conscious muscle movement of the hand controlling the changing direction of the pen. When this motion is relaxed, the strokes are automatically rounded and flow evenly. When there is stress or tension, this rhythm is disturbed, with the result that the movements of the pen are unco-ordinated, producing loops that vary in size, shape and formation.

Writing which has an even rhythm indicates harmony and inner balance, which can withstand strong external pressure, whereas writing that is unrhythmic and uneven, reveals an excitable and emotionally neurotic personality who is lacking

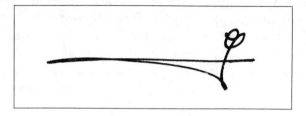

that inner balance. When the underlengths are extremely odd, eccentric or bizarre, they can reveal nervous disorders,

inhibitions, tension, sexual and physical disturbances or illness, aggressiveness, sadism, masochism, inflated sexual

fantasies and homosexuality in both male and female.

If the extension of the lower loop is long or short it reveals whether the instinctive drives are respectively deep or shallow. Round loops show imagination and emotionability and the pressure will show sensuality and energy – or lack of it – according to the thickness of the strokes.

The crossing of the downstroke by the upstroke is particularly significant, always taking into account that to the left slant shows introspection and an active inner life, and the right slant shows an extrovert and sociability.

The way in which the writer forms and crosses the *g* and *y* are indicative of his sexuality. How the writer deals with normal sexual relations, or if he lives in celibacy, self-imposed or otherwise, if he is impotent, or she is frigid, if there are homosexual tendencies or any form of unusual sexual behaviour will show clearly once the graphologist knows what to look for.

The downstroke also demonstrates if there are sadistic tendencies, aggressiveness, physical or mental weakness or resentfulness in the erotic/sexual area.

To understand these strokes it is necessary to study in some depth, many samples of handwriting, and it is dangerous for just one single g or y to be taken for proof of a feature. Although many traits that are abnormal may appear in handwriting, it does not always mean that the writer has practised abnormality or is even aware of it.

But the tendency is there and it could manifest itself sometime. It is true that the 'libido' (as defined by Freud) – the sex drive – can be seen in these lower loops, and so can specific sexual abnormalities.

Very often the male sexual organ can be seen in g and y as a sign of male homosexuality, and this is also seen in the handwriting of female inverts as a sexual symbol.

The regularity and irregularity of the size and formation of these two letters show the degree of receptability to stimulation and how the writer is going to respond. It is also a chart of emotional stability.

The varying loops and their formations reflect varying sexual preferences, and it must always be remembered that in forming these two letters, the natural movement is a downward one and then an upward swing. When the writer deviates from this procedure either by cutting off the crossing stroke, changing direction, or interrupting the motion and abruptly ending the stroke without crossing it, he is regulating the action and revealing some inhibition, repression or sexual quirk, even deficiency. Very large or inflated loops show a projection of sexual fantasy; strokes that do not follow the normal pattern show sexual functioning that is disorganised or evasive.

Normal sexuality

This is seen in well-rounded loops, generously long, and crossed at the top of the stem. It shows warmth of emotion, a normal physical desire, and an ability to give and receive love and affection. The pressure shows the writer's energy and vitality, while the fullness of the loop expresses depth of feeling and imagination.

Rounded strokes indicate non-aggressiveness towards and consideration for a partner, and a willingness to co-operate and share rather than dominate and use force.

The normal crossing stroke to the g and y is made by going straight down and crossing over to the right. The larger the loop the more emotional and the more vivid the imagination. The longer the downstroke, the more energy is shown.

Narrow or thin strokes are a sign of repressed or inhibited sexual desire, often caused by past emotional or environmental experiences that have left their mark. These may be due to religious scruples, moral conflict, or guilt, and result in anxiety.

Weak or trembling strokes are often a sign of illness, physical disability or age, but these traits must not be taken for impotence or frigidity, as they have different characteristics, caused not by sexual insufficiency but by physical ill-health and nervous exhaustion.

Sexual traits – good and bad

Loops within loops

These indicate compulsive behaviour which can become obsessive; they reveal persistence above the normal, and point to odd or quirky sexual interests. They also show writers who are stimulated by the visual and erotic, this loop is *not* to be confused with the female homosexual sign of the figure 8.

Huge exaggerated loops on the downstroke

These are a sign of a vivid imagination and an inflated ego, compensating for an inferiority complex. The writer indulges in sexual fantasy to make up for his lack of reality; he is usually boastful and theatrical in manner, needs to attract attention and admiration. He is often sexually disappointing but will talk about his triumphs (imaginary) and believes he projects an imagery of sexual excesses.

Broken loops

Any loop broken at the bottom is a sign of hidden fears and apprehensions about the sex act. The writer is conventionally correct and lives within a strict sexual code of behaviour.

A heavy unlooped downstroke thickening at the bottom of the stem

This shows the person who is emotionally dishonest and who may practise deceit in the sexual area by pretending to be something he is not and claiming to be sexually very active when he is not.

Exaggerated or inflated loops on other letters

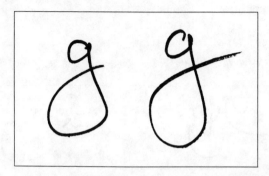

These indicate a highly developed sexual imagination, which often compensates for an inferiority complex – which may be seen also in huge capital letters.

Unfinished loops

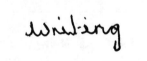

These, or loops which are slightly turned upwards, are a sign of sexual resignation, frigidity or impotence. But if the strokes are weak and without any vitality, there may be a physical reason or illness.

Large loops open to the left

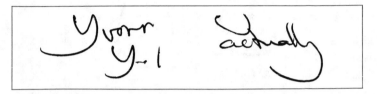

These are often seen in the handwriting of young girls and express emotional immaturity and impressionability. This loop also shows the writer who could be in love with love, or who has an incomplete sex life.

A straight line down

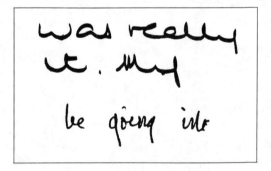

Used instead of a loop, this shows the writer who may sublimate sexual desire into other areas, using the energy in a business career, or home, and very often displaying good judgement and a fatalistic attitude to life. If the stroke is poor and weak, this again may be due to illness, fatigue or a lack of interest in sex.

The fantastic sized lower loop

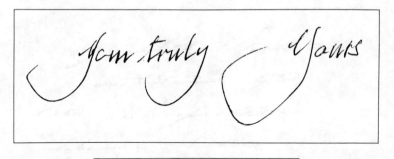

When it is exaggerated beyond reason, this reveals the writer's habit of letting his fantasy take over; he lacks reality in instinctive sex drive, resulting in powerful erotic day-dreaming. These strokes border on the idiosyncratic.

Very monotonous and regular lower loops

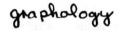

These can reveal a dull and poor temperament without imagination or sensitivity. They can also show repression of sexual urges and a degree of tension when they arise.

Long, weak and pushed-to-the-right downstroke

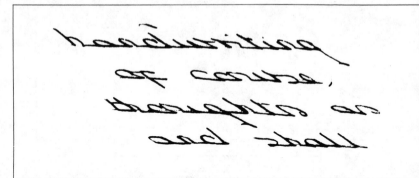

Aggression and obsessional neurosis is seen in this. The rest of the script indicates the rigid self-control the writer imposes on her emotional instincts. The small island at the foot of the loop shows that she is desperate to find security materialistically. Her inhibitions are the result of a very strong father influence.

Long, heavy and looped g

This along with pressure and slightly pasty appearance show strong physical desires and physical appetites.

Exaggerated and light pressured underlengths

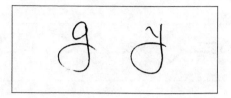

These are a sign of sensitivity, a vivid imagination and a tendency to magnify the truth at times due to a desire for attention and a need to show off. They reveal rather superficial feelings.

Triangular loops

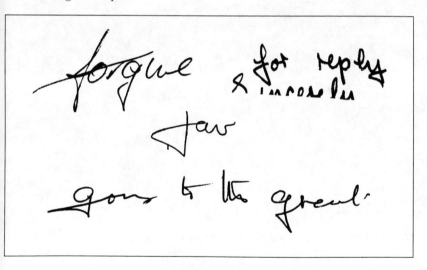

These are a sign of disappointment with the partner, and in female handwriting can also reveal the domestic tyrant. These angular loops are always seen in the script of people who find their partner sexually unsuitable or incompatible. This results in aggressiveness caused by frustration.

Narrow strokes, seldom looped

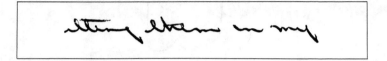

Impotence and frigidity are seen in narrow strokes or weak poorly formed strokes, sometimes ending abruptly and seldom looped. Where there is a loop, it is usually feeble and rarely crosses over the stem.

Clues to other proclivities

interests are my home, gardening
theatre and friends.
I want to find a good
friend who I can share my life with
and be good to. my telegram may
have given you the wrong impression
of me.

The raffle
party

The *grasping claw left* is a sign of an avoidance of responsibility, often sexual or emotional, and shows a materialistic nature, sometimes amounting to greed. The writer often has a money complex and may show more than a passing interest in hoarding for hoarding's sake. These writers are also clannish and have strong family feelings and ties.

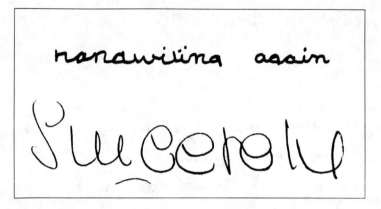

Where there is *no downstroke at all* and the writing is mainly in the middle zone, this shows the writer to be living in an emotional vacuum and may have a slightly schizoid personality, lacking in spiritual and emotional outlets. The feelings are directed into the home sphere and day-to-day matters rather than emotional needs.

Curled or enrolled underlengths show an abnormal sex interest and these writers are not always emotionally honest. They may be eccentric, holding odd ideas about sex.

A *very small loop at the end of the stem* shows the loner, the solitary person who is sexually frustrated and may indulge in mild deviations; this includes masturbation.

A *disproportionately long downstroke* in the lower zone betrays a desire for sexual satisfaction and a capacity for finding it.

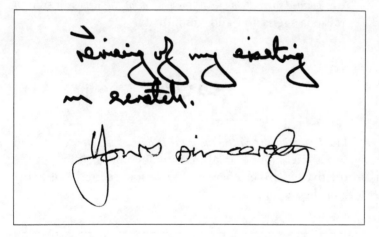

When the downstrokes are light and 'trembling', as seen in the hand of senile writers, it means their thoughts rarely lead to action.

Long loops with heavy pressure and *smudged or pasty appearance* show strong sex impulses, and appetites that are demanding and sensual. The animal or earthy approach to sex is near the surface and the writer is liable to be coarse and vulgar. When this dominant pressure is seen in large writing, it may point to manic depressive tendencies.

Narrow loops which go up the stem a little way but do not cross it, reveal sexual anxiety and irritability often the result of emotional frustration.

Any pointed or spiky angle at the bottom of the stem is a sign of repression, aggression and immaturity.

The *loop which is curled under the middle zone letter,* or is even non-existent, shows sexual inadequacy and a stifling of the instinctive sex drive. There can be various reasons, one being fear of the sex act.

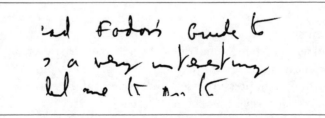

Small loops not crossing the stem show sexual anxiety and

repression due to weakness. The varying slant is a sign of
irritability and inconsistency emotionally.

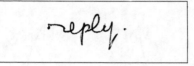

Short spiky underlengths going to the right are a sign of stifling of
the sex drive, sublimating it into spheres where the writer's
altruistic nature finds expression in social work and similar
constructive outlets.

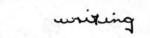

Short strokes going to the left are a sign of repression and sexual
immaturity, and a lack of imagination.

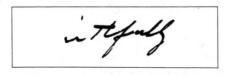

Tick-like strokes show sensitivity bordering on the neurotic
and aggressiveness. The writer directs his sex drives into
materialistic spheres rather than emotional release.

Weak, poorly formed and *neglected loops*, unfinished and

with open ovals, show anxiety and lack of sex drive due to anxiety.

Long and heavy pressured loops are a sign of the athlete and the sportsman; they show a love of physical fitness and activity and a down-to-earth healthy attitude to sex. Their approach to problems and day-to-day affairs is realistic. They are usually warm-hearted people who can show warmth towards the feelings of others and affection towards their loved ones.

When the loops vary in shape and size, they demonstrate a changeable and inconsistent nature, restlessness and moodiness, sometimes emotional instability.

Know³ will bring light in His good time – sometimes we have to 'wait on the Lord + be of good courage'. – That text was sent to me + I gave up hope "of" finding Gerda – my little dog. When I was at my end of hope, that I had a message all was well. So dear souls keep up courage. – "I, for one altho my feeble efforts, will

These oddly shaped *g's spiked at the top with a curly bottom* reveal conflict between the spiritual and the sexual. The writer cannot come to terms with her physical needs so channels a lot of her energies into the occult, compensating for her unfulfilled needs.

The capital *B* is a sexual symbol and the heavy pressure of the writing here shows intensity of emotion which is unable to find expression in the normal way owing to her disturbed disposition.

> *you to make an assessment of my ~~~~~ ~~~~~~*
>
> *You really are a most beautiful woman and I have had glorious fantasy dreams of you, when my head is floating beneath your diaphanous negligee with my lips sensuously in contact with the lovely sweep of your thigh just above your calf.*
>
> *In ecstasy my lips gently and slowly travel over your beautiful soft white skin and go mad as they reach the soft, warmer more wonderful areas of your upper thighs*
>
> *My head, floats nearer to the most divine part of your heavenly body, my senses are aflame with desire and longing and hunger to satisfy, my most tender ~~~~~*

These *twisted and ill-formed loops* show unusual sexual fantasies, a pre-occupation with the instinctive drives, and an inflated sexual imagination, due to inadequacy.

This man gets his kicks by writing anonymous letters of a sexual nature, and reading pornography. He has a strange and strong compulsion, and he is unable to cope with his sexuality, possibly owing to a dominant mother in his early life, and this can be seen in the long swing back to the left.

This *long narrow downstroke* reveals a withholding of the sexual instincts and the contracting strokes indicate inhibition and the holding in check of strong emotional desires. The heavy pressure points to plenty of energy and a writer who is sensual, but together these show suffering from tension that restricts the normal sex life and reveals pent up emotion and even anger.

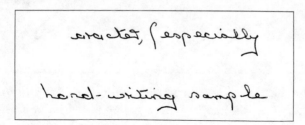

This very *light and slightly left-slanting* script with its *low-slung underlengths,* reveals that the writer cuts off her instinctive drives and avoids involvement in sex. This stroke is also associated with money and a liking for the material things in life. The light pressure applied to the underlengths shows hypersensitivity and a critical streak.

Strange and weird are the fantasies shown in this writer's *angular and aggressive downstrokes*. Even the letter *f* and the capital *G* which are distorted, show resentment. There is a tendency here to indulge in odd sexual behaviour and, although the writer is male, he has many feminine traits – this writing is sometimes seen in the script of transvestites.

These extraordinary strokes swooping first left and to the right, *hooklike and sharp*, reveal a strong father influence. The writer is intolerant and cannot leave the instinctive drive area where a lot of her fantasies are materialistic. This is often a sign of avarice, suspicion and a refusal to come into too close emotional contact. The strong ego accented by this grasping hook is often the result of emotional deceit and a desire to compensate for sexual inadequacy. Her fantasies spill over into her world of reality and there are paranoid trends here.

the foggy foggy

These *sickle-like strokes* formed in an open circle are a sign of aggression and resentment, the writer with her left slant is introverted, resentful and her sexual fantasies are often obsessional.

thfully

This *tiny tick-like stroke* at the end of the stem is a sign of frustration and repression. The writer has weak sex impulses and little vitality for coping with normally instinctive drives.

The *t* bar makes *a religious cross* and this is very often found in the handwriting of people who are inhibited through living in their early days in a restricted or highly repressive environment. It shows unfulfilled emotional needs.

get together

This *short underlength* indicates a lack of drive and of immaturity in the emotional area. The writer is clannish, dependent and, from the unrhythmic script, rather nervous and suffering from anxiety.

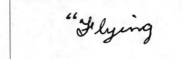

These *light-pressured* and *poorly formed underlengths* show a lack of vitality, that the writer is frigid and has little interest in sex.

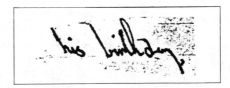

This *long downstroke* with its *right swing* and *tiny hook halfway up the stem* shows a father influence, while the general left slant of the writing reveals a very introverted nature. The writer has difficulty in establishing relationships because of being so withdrawn.

This *straight line down* shows signs of a devitalised personality, and yet the writing is quite good and appears well balanced, by cutting off the sex drive the writer shows that she lives in voluntary or enforced chastity.

Sensuality

Sensuality is seen in heavy pressure applied to the *g* and *y*, especially on the downstroke which is usually looped and long.

Pressure shows the amount of energy used to glide the pen over the paper. It symbolises the libido, the mental and physical drives that produce activity. It can reveal the state of health, vitality, feelings and sensuality of the writer; if there is little pressure in the script, there is little energy. When the pressure varies in loops, something is not right. It could be sexual maladjustment due to the sex drive being channelled or sublimated into other spheres.

Very often extreme sensuality is expressed by smudgy or 'pasty' script, revealing that the writer is easily aroused and has strong sexual desires when excited, sometimes possessing a sensuality that borders on animal lust, and coupled with a lack of spirituality. This is particularly so where the script is slow and of copybook form level. Among really sensual handwriting we find the rapist and the brutally aggressive.

The whole emotional pattern of the handwriting when seen is of a muddy appearance and the slant is often wildly angled to the right. Violence is associated with this particular loop and if the stroke persists in pressure and size all through the writing, the animal instincts are very close to the surface. Such writers are selfish, lustful and lacking in consideration for their partners. Self-gratification is their motto. They will have a lowered resistance to perversions and excesses. When the downstroke is angular as well, there is a desire to dominate. Handwriting with filled-in small letters and blots here and there, shows pre-occupation with anal erotica.

Father influence

This thin narrow tick-like stroke at the bottom and its swing to the right, indicates a strong father influence and is a sign of repressed sexuality due to inhibitions in early life.

This small copybook form-level script with its cut-off lower loops, shows the writer to be repressing her sexual inclinations, and because of the swing to the left of her *g*'s and *y*'s she cannot let go of early influences and experiences. There is no compelling instinctive drive here at all.

Depression

Long narrow loops indicate tension and sexual frustration and often emotion is held in check. The writer has difficulty in coping with his feelings and becomes disorganised and unable to sustain relationships.

A narrow and compressed *g* or *y* or a stem that has no loop at all reveals a poor imagination and lack of warmth. The writer is inhibited and is nearly always under some form of tension which restricts emotional release.

Impotence and frigidity

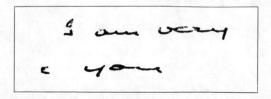

This narrow, poorly made downstroke indicates sexual inadequacy and frigidity. The light pressure reveals physical weakness and little interest in sex.

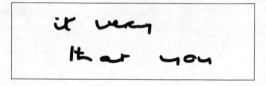

This very wide script with its neglected underlengths shows a passive, non-aggressive, matter-of-fact personality, in whom physical desire is almost non-existent. The writer is a 'bluffer' where her feelings are concerned, and the thickening base at the end of the stem indicates she may be a flirt, showing an apparently affectionate response to emotional overtures, but who in reality is putting up a façade. She enjoys the chase but not the capture.

> would make things a lot easier. Although it
> embarrassing and hard to do than having another row, and
> better afterwards.

Middle-zone handwriting without any upper or lower loops show this writer to be living in a vacuum. She has no interest in the spiritual or sexual, and the rigidity of her writing and small neglected lower loops show that she is afraid of emotional involvement. There are also signs of neurotic obsessional behaviour, and the writer cannot 'give' sexually but channels her energies into home and day-to-day affairs.

Male homosexuality

Male homosexuality is revealed in a small *g* and *y* that sweeps to the left. This is the Oedipus Complex symbol in graphology and shows a strong attachment to the mother figure.

It is expressed by the loop, long or inflated, that is pushed to the left, or stroke that shifts to the left with a horizontal stroke across. This particular sign may also be in evidence in the capital *J*.

When the pull to the left is strongly marked, this is also an indication of introspection and that the libido is turned inwards resulting in a degree of narcissism.

Many denominators of the homosexual as seen in handwriting, are also signs of emotional immaturity and sensitivity.

I am really looking forward
to seeing you at the weekend.

Tommy

maybe we can get together soon and our meeting will be mutually exciting for future meetings to become a regular thing

John.

imagine what you look like but I'm luck Perhaps your got a no waist a bald head and hairy

housing prices will rise a little! If
its suitable words of praise, I may
ugh, this seems unlikely — just my

ave dancing Reading writing ona
if you are instead and not Colour
re we could become good friends If you.
? explan more in my nex letter all the

Female homosexuality

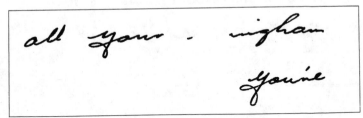

Female homosexuality is often revealed in the way the *g* or *y* is formed in the shape of the figure *8*. This twisted downstroke may also appear at times in male homosexual writing.

It indicates deviation from the normal but does not always mean that the writer is aware of unusual sexual tendencies. It

Gracious Lord O bomb the Germans.
Spare their women for thy sake,
And if that is not so easy,
We will pardon thy mistake

is difficult to establish from this stroke if the writer is active or passive, usually the pressure if heavy together with a long downstroke, will betray depth of feeling.

graphol og

Please let me know about picking up scripts.

Thanks!

The figure *8* is also found in the handwriting of people who have literary talent. Another female homosexual sign is the loop that swings to the left – a sexual symbol of the male organ.

Extremely strong desires are shown in this *twisted 8* belonging to a female homosexual. The pointed base is a sign of some aggression and the pressure reveals energy and vitality. Materialism and abnormal sexual instincts are shown in a way that even the untutored graphological eye would realise that this writer has some quirk of personality in her make-up.

Other sexual traits

The *long downstroke* with its *turned up angular stroke* reveals aggression and stunted sexual desire, as indicated in the way the t-bars are formed in a cross sign, showing strong guilt feelings and repression due to an early religious background.

This right-slanted script with *left pushed underlengths* and *hooklike arched and long strokes*, point together to an avoidance of responsibility in the emotional area. This writer cannot cut the links and ties that bind her to past experiences – especially emotional and sexual influences.

These curiously *rounded figure 8* symbols belong to a male homosexual and reveal his feminine instincts with desire for harmony and domesticity in the sexual area. When this particular sign is seen in female handwriting, it often belongs to the woman who wishes for a child, very often in vain. . . .

Inferiority complex

This writer feels the need to compensate for a sense of inferiority, so exaggerates his capitals and inflates the loops and strokes in an almost bizarre way. This is a bid for attention and admiration and reveals a deep seated need for recognition.

The writer has a pronounced ego but lacks real self-confidence, so hides this with what he considers to be 'different' script which catches attention. What he is also doing is revealing a lack of taste and intelligence. Abnormally large capitals are usually the mask under which he hides his lack of assurance.

Aggression

parents on Friday afternoon as I had been in
trouble. I dont know what came over me but
during first lesson Today I got Mr Manning & threated
73 him with I knife at the same time demand
money. I funked it up the west-end but got
nervous so I got in touch with Ted a lad in Keyton
stone. When I arrived two C.I.D. men were there
& took me to Woodford police Station and
73 took a statement from me which my Dad
had to sign. Mr Green has expelled me from
St. Pauls and it might be weeks before I
can get into another school. The Juvinile court
might take weeks to come to a desicion.
73 I might be let off with a warning or
yet looked I might have to leave home for
a little while.

This erratic and varying slant shows mood variation and a
neurotic personality. The writer is a young man with a strict
religious background who reveals latent aggression and an
inferiority complex. The spiritual pressure on him is seen in
the form of the cross in his t-bar, and his sense of inferiority in
the smallness of his capital *I*.

Anger is shown in the thin narrow strokes and absence of
loops in his script, indicating emotional repression. His
neurotic personality comes through in the constant amend-
ments and touching up of letters.

Sexual fantasy

When other sexual symbols appear constantly in hand-writing, they are an indication of the writer's pre-occupation with the sexual organs.

Sometimes they indicate a leaning to perversions or other abnormal forms of sexual behaviour.

The most common sexual symbols frequently found in the capital letters are in the *B W* and *P*. This is because parts of the human anatomy are seen in these letters which reflect the writer's tendencies, obsessions and even compulsions.

Sadism, masochism and mental cruelty

Mental cruelty can be seen in sharp, spiky downstrokes and long whiplike strokes that end in angular or lash-like pointed

My only reason for getting

touch with your magazine

is that I wouldn't

knowing that yours

be at the following charges today.

ends. This shows the writer who will use calculated mental cruelty to subdue others to get his own way. It is rare for these strokes to be seen in female handwriting.

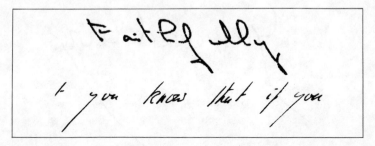

These very long strokes denote a pre-occupation with the instinctual. The sexual urges are strong but lacking in imagination, kindness, warmth or affection.

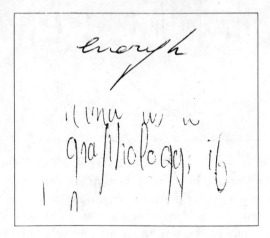

When the downstroke is abnormally thin, this can be due to fear or inhibition, the writer is fearful that his personality will suffer if he expresses his emotional needs in the normal way.

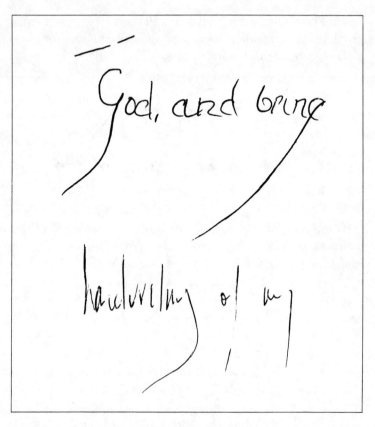

Sadism is revealed by whiplike lashes to the downstrokes and upstrokes, and by narrow, angular and repressed writing without any loops or rounded formations.

Sometimes sadistic and masochistic writers will have symbols of knives, daggers and arrows as well. Such symbols are seen in the handwriting of violent people whose mind and imagination lingers on such things. Sometimes too, these symbols, with others, are a pointer to suicidal tendencies.

Aleister Crowley

Reputed to have been the wickedest man in England during the 'Thirties, Crowley was a drug addict and a practitioner of the black arts, being a priest of black masses. Two of his wives died insane and he was alleged to have driven several of his mistresses to suicide.

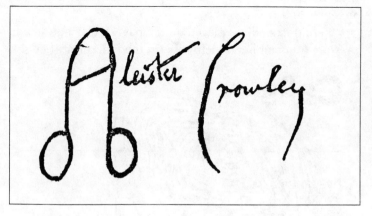

His signature with the abnormally strong downstrokes going into the lower zone (note his capital *A*) shows his preoccupation with the elemental instinctive drives, an inflated sexual imagination, and leaning to perversions.

The sabre-like strokes to his capital *C* and small *y* indicate sadistic tendencies, while the heavy pressure is a sign of his energy and sensuality.

The whole signature shows exaggerated sexual urges and excesses.

Doodles and sexual symbolism

Doodle symbolism is often used by psychologists to understand the subconscious because these 'nonsense pictures', as they are sometimes known, reveal obvious fears and hopes, anxieties and dreams.

Where the doodle is placed on the page, its formation and pressure all combine to help discern the innermost thoughts

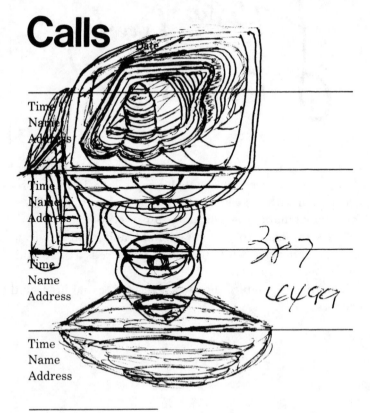

Male doodle

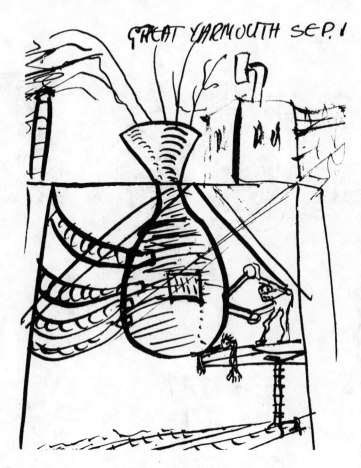

Female doodle

and desires of the writer, and help a consultant to bring to the surface any inner conflicts.

Sexual doodles can be divided into male and female. Male doodles are more likely to take the form of, for example, shoes or legs, the female form and the use of angular strokes and formations, while female doodles are of snakes, faces, fish, circles, plants and flowers which represent the reproductive organs and fertility.

The male who has little experience of girls will often doodle parts of the female form or doodles showing preoccupation with war and aggression, while young girls who are in love with love will draw hearts, flowers and circular formations of groups of stars or leaves, representing sexual longings and children.

Above: Female doodle
Right: Male doodle

Above: Male doodle
Right: Female doodles

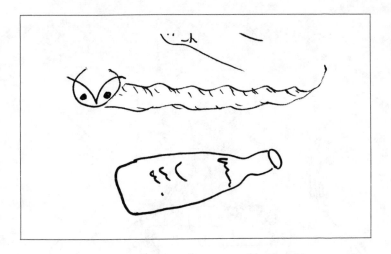

1. This doodle is the most common form of sexual doodle drawn by older people and its sexual significance is obvious. It is basically non-aggressive and a graphic symbol of withdrawal and unfulfilled desire.

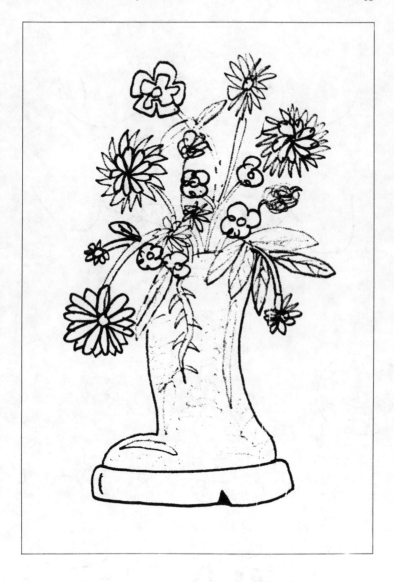

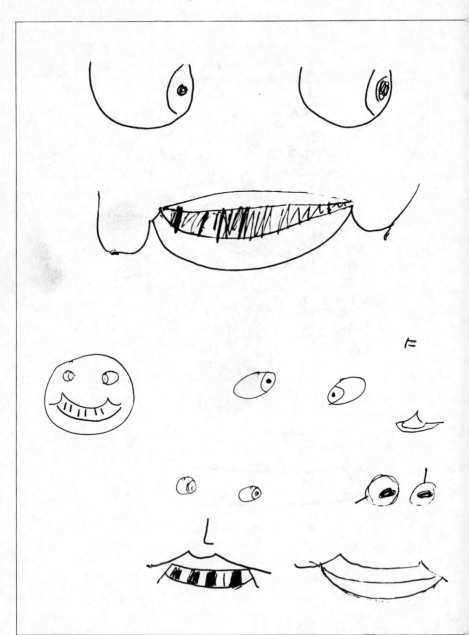

2. The watching eye and teeth or the mouth are often seen in the doodles of male homosexuals and are associated with anxiety and often worry about sex, also occasionally jealousy, and a fear of the opposite sex.

3. This shows a little pent up anxiety. Filling in of a doodle is a sign of some apprehension – the heavier the pressure of the filling in, the more conflict the writer is experiencing and is a sign that the writer is seeking the solution to an emotional problem.

4. Doodles of shoes and feet have sexual undertones and are well-known projections of male fantasies, and reveal a preoccupation with the instinctive drives.

5. This somewhat unusual doodle reveals the writer's need to have a wish fulfilled; to be the all-pervading male, and illustrates his feeling of inadequacy knowing that this will never be achieved.

Bibliography

JACOBY, H.J. *Analysis of Handwriting*, George Allen & Unwin. 1939.

MARCUSE, IRENE, *Applied Graphology*, Macoy Publishing Co., 1946.

MENDEL, ALFRED O, *Personality in Handwriting*, Stephen Daye Press, 1974.

ROMAN, K.G., *Handwriting, A Key to Personality*, Routledge & Kegan Paul, 1954.

SAUDEK, ROBERT, *The Psychology of Handwriting*, George Allen & Unwin, 1925.

SINGER ERIC, *A Manual of Graphology*, Duckworth, 1969.

SONNERMANN, ULRICH, *Handwriting Analysis*, Grune and Stratton, 1950.

JUNG, CARL, *Four Archetypes*, Routledge & Kegan Paul, 1972.

JUNG, CARL, *Man and his Symbols*, Aldus Books, 1964.

WOLF, WERNER, *Diagrams of the Unconscious* Grune & Stratton, 1948.

OLYANOVA, NADYA, *The Psychology of Handwriting*, Sterling Publishing Co., 1960.